Personal Finance and Budgeting

Table of Contents

1. The Basics of Personal Finance

(1) - 1.1 Understanding Income and Expenses

(2) - 1.2 The Importance of Financial Literacy

(3) - 1.3 Key Financial Terms Everyone Should Know

2. Setting Financial Goals

(1) - 2.1 Short-term vs. Long-term Financial Goals

(2) - 2.2 SMART Goals Framework for Financial Planning

(3) - 2.3 Prioritizing Your Financial Objectives

3. Creating a Budget

(1) - 3.1 Different Budgeting Methods Explained

(2) - 3.2 How to Track Monthly Expenses

(3) - 3.3 Adjusting Your Budget for Life Changes

4. Managing Debt

(1) - 4.1 Types of Debt: Good vs. Bad

(2) - 4.2 Strategies for Paying Off Debt

(3) - 4.3 The Role of Credit Scores in Financial Health

5. Saving Strategies

(1) - 5.1 Building an Emergency Fund

(2) - 5.2 High-Interest Savings Accounts vs. Regular Accounts

(3) - 5.3 Automating Your Savings

6. Understanding Investments

(1) - 6.1 The Basics of Stocks, Bonds, and Mutual Funds

(2) - 6.2 Investment Risks and Rewards

(3) - 6.3 How to Start Investing as a Beginner

7. Retirement Planning

(1) - 7.1 Why Start Early with Retirement Savings

(2) - 7.2 Types of Retirement Accounts Explained

(3) - 7.3 Calculating Your Retirement Needs

8. Insurance and Protection

(1) - 8.1 Types of Insurance You Need

(2) - 8.2 Assessing Your Insurance Needs

(3) - 8.3 Understanding Deductibles and Premiums

9. Tax Planning Basics

(1) - 9.1 Understanding Your Tax Bracket

(2) - 9.2 Deductions and Credits You Should Know

(3) - 9.3 Tax-Advantaged Accounts and Their Benefits

10. Financial Tools and Apps

(1) - 10.1 Best Budgeting Apps for Personal Finance

(2) - 10.2 Using Spreadsheets for Budgeting

(3) - 10.3 Online Tools for Tracking Investments

11. Building Wealth Over Time

(1) - 11.1 The Power of Compound Interest

(2) - 11.2 Diversifying Your Investment Portfolio

(3) - 11.3 Real Estate as an Investment Option

12. Navigating Financial Crises

(1) - 12.1 Creating a Financial Crisis Plan

(2) - 12.2 Communicating About Money with Family

(3) - 12.3 Resources for Financial Assistance

13. The Role of Financial Advisors

(1) - 13.1 When to Consider Hiring a Financial Advisor

(2) - 13.2 Understanding Different Fee Structures

(3) - 13.3 Questions to Ask a Potential Advisor

14. Financial Independence and Early Retirement (FIRE)

(1) - 14.1 Key Concepts Behind FIRE

(2) - 14.2 Strategies for Achieving Financial Independence

(3) - 14.3 Potential Challenges and How to Overcome Them

15. Continuous Financial Education

(1) - 15.1 Resources for Ongoing Learning

(2) - 15.2 Importance of Staying Updated on Financial Trends

(3) - 15.3 Building a Network for Financial Growth

1. The Basics of Personal Finance

1.1 Understanding Income and Expenses

Income can take many forms, and it's essential to recognize the various sources that contribute to your financial wellbeing. Primarily, most people derive their income from wages, which is the amount paid to them for their work. This can come from a regular salary or hourly wages calculated based on the hours worked. Beyond basic wages, many individuals also receive bonuses, which are one-time payments often linked to performance, and can significantly boost overall earnings. In addition to these, passive income plays a crucial role in diversifying income streams. Passive income refers to earnings that come without actively working for them, such as rental income from properties, dividends from investments, or royalties from creative works. By understanding and monitoring your various income sources, you can get a clearer picture of your financial landscape and make informed decisions about budgeting and saving.

On the other hand, managing expenses is equally vital in the equation of personal finance. Expenses can be broadly categorized into two types: fixed and variable. Fixed expenses are costs that remain constant each month, regardless of how much you earn or spend. This includes items like rent or mortgage payments, insurance, and certain bills. Understanding these fixed costs is crucial because they represent the baseline amount you need to earn to maintain your lifestyle. Conversely, variable expenses fluctuate depending on your personal choices and activities. This category includes things like groceries, entertainment, and utilities, which can vary each month. By distinguishing between these types of expenses, you can gain better control over your finances, allowing you to adjust your spending habits as needed. This understanding helps you allocate your resources more effectively, setting you on a path toward achieving financial goals.

To improve your budgeting skills, consider tracking both your income and expenses meticulously. Using apps or simple spreadsheets can help in recording each transaction, providing you with insights into your spending habits. This practice not only highlights areas where you might cut back but also reveals patterns in your income that you can capitalize on. The more informed you are about your financial flow—both incoming and outgoing—the better equipped you'll be to make sound financial decisions that enhance your overall economic health.

1.2 The Importance of Financial Literacy

Financial literacy essentially means having the knowledge and skills to manage your financial resources effectively. It encompasses understanding various aspects of money management, including budgeting, saving, investing, and making informed decisions about loans and credit. In today's complex financial landscape, being financially literate is critical. Individuals need to grasp how financial systems work, from interest rates to investment vehicles, to navigate their financial journeys successfully. This understanding plays a vital role in personal finance management, empowering individuals to set realistic goals, control their spending, and plan for the future. The more educated one becomes about finances, the better equipped they are to handle unexpected expenses and avoid falling into debt traps.

Being financially literate can lead to significant long-term advantages that profoundly impact your life. One of the most notable benefits is the ability to make better savings and investment decisions. When you are knowledgeable about financial concepts, you are more likely to create and stick to a budget that reflects your priorities and goals. This knowledge also equips you to diversify your investments effectively, buy into high-performance assets, and make calculations about risk versus reward. Moreover, financially literate individuals might also find themselves less vulnerable to financial scams or predatory lending practices. An understanding of how to evaluate the terms of a loan or a credit card can save you from overpaying and incurring hidden fees. Ultimately, this education leads to greater financial stability and independence, allowing you to focus on building a prosperous future.

Improving your financial literacy can start with simple steps, such as reading finance-related books and articles, attending workshops, or online courses. The more you learn and practice your skills, the more confident you'll become in managing your finances.

1.3 Key Financial Terms Everyone Should Know

Understanding finance can feel overwhelming, but familiarizing yourself with some common financial terminology can make a significant difference. Assets are everything you own that have value, from cash and stocks to your home and car. Liabilities, on the other hand, represent what you oweâ€"like loans, credit card debts, and mortgages. Cash flow is crucial for managing your finances; it's the movement of money in and out of your accounts, showing how much cash you have available. Positive cash flow means you have more money coming in than going out, which is essential for building savings or making investments. On the flip side, negative cash flow indicates you're spending more than you earn, which can lead to financial difficulties.

Alongside these foundational terms, it's beneficial to know a few key concepts found in the finance world. Terms like ROI, or Return on Investment, are frequently used to indicate how much profit or loss you're making on an investment relative to its cost. Another important term is liquidity, which refers to how easily an asset can be converted into cash without significantly affecting its value. When you hear the term â€œdiversification,â€• it refers to spreading your investments across various assets to lower risk. Understanding acronyms such as APR (Annual Percentage Rate) will also help you navigate loans and credit cards, as it gives you insight into how much interest you'll pay over time. These terms, among others, form the backbone of personal finance knowledge.

To build a solid foundation for your financial literacy, take the time to understand these concepts, and donâ€™t hesitate to dig deeper into any terms that confuse you. Regularly updating your knowledge about basic financial terms can help you make informed decisions, whether you're budgeting, investing, or planning for retirement. When you encounter financial documents or discussions that include these terms, having a good grasp of what they mean will empower you to engage with the material and improve your financial situation effectively.

2. Setting Financial Goals

2.1 Short-term vs. Long-term Financial Goals

Identifying short-term financial goals is crucial for maintaining a healthy budget and achieving a sense of immediate accomplishment. These goals typically have a timeframe of less than one year and can include objectives such as saving for a vacation, purchasing new appliances, or building an emergency fund. The key to setting these goals is to make them specific, measurable, attainable, relevant, and time-bound, often referred to as SMART criteria. For instance, instead of vague aspirations like "I want to save money," it's more effective to say "I want to save $3,000 for a vacation by next December." This way, you have a clear target to aim for, making it easier to track your progress and stay motivated.

Planning for long-term financial goals is equally important as these aspirations can span several years or even decades. Common long-term goals include saving for retirement, purchasing a home, or funding a child's education. Understanding how to set these goals ensures you can strategically allocate your resources over time. Start by assessing your current financial situation and envisioning where you want to be in the future. For example, if your target is to retire by age 65 with a comfortable nest egg, calculate how much you need to save monthly to reach that goal. This long-range planning may include contributing to retirement accounts, understanding compound interest, and adjusting your budget to prioritize these savings. Establishing long-term goals provides a framework that can guide your short-term spending and saving decisions.

The journey toward financial stability is made up of both short-term and long-term goals. Each has distinct advantages that can help you navigate your financial landscape. A practical tip is to regularly review and update your financial goals. As life circumstances change—such as a new job, a move, or family dynamics—you may need to adjust your approach. This practice encourages adaptive management of your finances, ensuring that you remain on track to achieve all your financial aspirations, both near and far.

2.2 SMART Goals Framework for Financial Planning

Specific, Measurable, Achievable, Relevant, Time-bound—these five principles form the backbone of the SMART criteria, which is essential for setting effective financial goals. Specificity is crucial; when planning your financial future, you should clearly define what you want to achieve. Instead of saying, I want to save money, articulate it as, I want to save $5,000 for a vacation. Measurable goals allow you to track progress; determining increments, such as saving $500 each month, gives you a concrete way to monitor advancement. Achievability is about setting realistic goals. While aiming high is important, your goals should still be within reach considering your financial situation and current obligations. Relevance makes sure your financial goals align with your broader life objectives—ask yourself how this goal will impact your life and if it resonates with what you truly value. Finally, a time-bound goal comes with a deadline, turning your vision into a plan. Setting a timeframe, like "I will save $5,000 by next June," helps maintain focus and accountability.

Creating SMART financial goals requires practice, but the results are worth the effort. For instance, if you wish to improve your credit score, a SMART goal might look like this: "I will increase my credit score by 50 points in six months by making all my payments on time, reducing my credit utilization to below 30%, and monitoring my credit report monthly for inaccuracies." This goal is specific (increase credit score), measurable (50 points), achievable (considering your current score), relevant (improving financial health), and time-bound (six months). Another example might involve saving for retirement: "I will contribute 15% of my monthly salary to my retirement account for the next year to build a financial cushion for my future.â€• This clearly defined goal aligns with long-term plans, is easy to track, and has a specified timeframe, making it a practical approach to retirement savings.

The key to applying the SMART framework is to ensure that each goal is interlinked with your overall financial strategy. Consider all aspects of your financial lifeâ€"from budgeting and debt reduction to investment goals and emergency savings. When you define your goals within the SMART criteria, you create a structured pathway for financial growth. Remember, the clearer your goals, the more likely youâ€™ll achieve them. A practical tip to integrate into your financial planning is to regularly revisit and adjust your goals as life circumstances change, keeping them aligned with your current situation and aspirations.

2.3 Prioritizing Your Financial Objectives

Assessing your financial goals begins with a clear understanding of your current situation. Start by listing out all your financial objectives, whether it's saving for a house, planning for retirement, funding education, or simply enjoying travel. Once you have a comprehensive list, consider your immediate needs versus long-term aspirations. Immediate needs may include paying off debt or building an emergency fund, while goals like retirement savings can often take a back seat. A method that works well is categorizing your goals into short-term, mid-term, and long-term. This prioritization allows you to focus on what is urgent versus what is important and often helps clarify which financial endeavors will provide the most benefit now versus later.

Life is unpredictable, and circumstances change, which means your financial priorities might need to adjust. Major life events such as job changes, marriage, having children, or moving can significantly impact your financial landscape. Regularly reassess your goals to ensure they align with your current situation. For example, if you get a promotion, your financial priorities might shift, enabling you to save more towards long-term goals. Keeping a monthly check-in on your goals can help you gauge where to allocate resources effectively. Moreover, leveraging tools like budgeting apps can aid in this process, providing you insights into your spending habits and available savings to adjust your priorities as needed.

It's also beneficial to remain flexible and open-minded in your financial journey. You may encounter unforeseen expenses, or your aspirations might evolve as you progress through different life stages. Adapting to these changes doesn't mean abandoning your goals; it means staying proactive about your financial health. For instance, if your travel plans change due to work commitments, you might redirect those funds toward enhancing your emergency savings instead. Remember, your financial objectives are not set in stone; they should evolve with you. By staying informed and adaptable, you can make the right financial choices that suit your lifestyle and aspirations.

3. Creating a Budget

3.1 Different Budgeting Methods Explained

Zero-based budgeting is a powerful method that requires you to plan for every dollar of your income. Instead of simply tracking what you earn and what you spend, this approach pushes you to assign every single dollar to specific expenses and savings. This means that at the end of the month, your income minus your expenses and savings should equal zero. It encourages intentional spending, making you accountable for every financial decision you make. For instance, if your monthly income is $3,000, you would detail how you'll use that entire amount. You could allocate $1,500 for rent, $300 for groceries, $200 for utilities, $500 for savings, and the remainder for discretionary spending. This clarity can significantly help you prioritize your financial goals, whether it's building an emergency fund, paying off debts, or saving for future investments.

The 50/30/20 rule presents another straightforward budgeting method. This strategy divides your income into three categories: needs, wants, and savings. According to this rule, 50% of your income should go towards needs, which includes essential expenses like housing, food, transportation, and healthcare. The next 30% is allocated to wants, such as dining out, entertainment, and vacations—essentially, non-essentials that enhance your life but are not required. The final 20% is designated for savings and debt repayment. This clear-cut division helps streamline your financial planning, making it easier to manage your money while still enjoying your lifestyle. For example, if you earn $4,000 a month, you would budget $2,000 for needs, $1,200 for wants, and $800 for savings. This strategy ensures you're meeting your fundamental needs, enjoying life, and preparing for the future all at once.

Understanding these budgeting methods can greatly enhance your personal finance management. Whether you choose the detailed approach of zero-based budgeting or the percentage allocation of the 50/30/20 rule, the goal is to empower you to take control of your financial situation. A useful tip to remember is to review and adjust your budget regularly. Life changes—like salary increases or unexpected expenses—can impact your financial plan. Stay flexible and adjust your spending habits as necessary to keep alignment with your goals.

3.2 How to Track Monthly Expenses

Choosing the right method to track your monthly expenses can significantly impact your financial awareness. There are numerous tools and strategies available, so it's crucial to find one that aligns with your lifestyle and preferences. Many people today take advantage of budgeting apps, as they can easily sync with your bank accounts and credit cards, helping you categorize spending automatically. Examples include Mint, YNAB (You Need A Budget), and PocketGuard. If you prefer a more hands-on approach, you might opt for a traditional notebook or ledger. This method could provide a tangible sense of your spending, allowing you to jot down purchases in real time. Another effective strategy is the envelope system, which involves allocating a specific amount of cash for various spending categories each month. By physically separating your money, you can avoid overspending in any particular area. Whatever method you choose, the key is consistency and making sure it fits seamlessly into your daily routine.

Once you have tracked your expenses for a month or two, it becomes essential to review those spending habits regularly. This process is not merely about looking at numbers; it provides an opportunity to reflect on your financial choices and identify areas where adjustments might be necessary. Start by looking for spending patterns. Are there categories where you consistently overspend? Perhaps dining out or entertainment is taking a bigger bite out of your budget than you realized. Recognizing these patterns can foster more mindful spending. Additionally, reviewing your expenses can highlight opportunities for savings, such as subscriptions you no longer use or services you can downgrade. It's also important to reassess your financial goals periodically. As circumstances change, your spending plan should adapt to accommodate new needs or priorities. This practice not only enhances your financial discipline but also empowers you to take control of your financial future.

To make the most of your tracking and reviews, consider setting aside a specific time each month to dive into your finances. This dedicated time allows you to focus without distractions, making the task less daunting. Utilize this time not just to review past spending but also to plan for the upcoming month. By anticipating expenses, such as birthdays or annual bills, you can better allocate your budget. Remember, the goal of tracking isn't just to limit spending but also to help you make informed financial decisions that support your overall well-being. Establishing a clear awareness of your expenses is the first step towards achieving financial stability.

3.3 Adjusting Your Budget for Life Changes

Recognizing life events that can trigger a need to review your budget is an essential skill. Major changes such as a job transition, marriage, divorce, the birth of a child, or even moving to a new home can significantly impact your financial landscape. For instance, starting a new job might come with changes in salary, benefits, or even commuting costs that weren't part of your previous financial plan. Similarly, if you're welcoming a new family member, whether it's a baby or a relative moving in, you will likely face increased expenses, such as childcare, education, or simply the cost of raising another person. Understanding these pivotal moments in your life can help you recognize when it's time to take a fresh look at your financial situation.

Flexibility in budgeting is crucial as it allows you to remain on top of your finances amidst changing circumstances. You should approach your budget as a living document that you can adjust as necessary. If you experience a rise or fall in income, such as a promotion, a new job, or even temporary unemployment, you should promptly reflect this in your budget. Similarly, try to account for unexpected expenses that may arise from life changes, such as medical bills or home repairs. Building a cushion in your budget for these fluctuations can reduce the stress associated with financial uncertainties. Moreover, setting aside a portion of your budget for discretionary spending can provide breathing room, ensuring that you do not feel deprived while still maintaining control over your financial goals.

Life changes will always happen, and being prepared financially can help you manage these shifts more easily. Regularly reviewing your budget—ideally on a monthly basis—ensures you stay aware of where your money is going and allows you to make informed decisions that align with your current life situation. One practical tip is to create a dedicated line item in your budget for life changes—it could be a small percentage of your income allocated to accommodate whatever new expenses may come your way. This proactive measure not only helps you handle the financial aspects of unforeseen events but also instills a sense of confidence that you can take on whatever life throws at you.

4. Managing Debt

4.1 Types of Debt: Good vs. Bad

Good debt refers to borrowing that can lead to financial growth and investment opportunities. This type of debt is typically an investment in your future, creating avenues for wealth-building. For instance, student loans, when used wisely, can enable you to earn a higher degree and secure better job prospects. Similarly, mortgages can be seen as good debt because they allow individuals to purchase homes that tend to appreciate over time, leading to equity build-up. Business loans also represent good debt, as they can provide the necessary capital to start or expand a business, generating income that far exceeds the cost of the loan. The key to leveraging good debt lies in ensuring that the return on investment is greater than the cost of the debt itself.

Bad debt, on the other hand, is often characterized by high-interest rates and does not contribute to wealth creation. High-interest credit card debt is a common example, as it can spiral out of control quickly if not managed properly. This type of borrowing often stems from consumer spending on non-essential items that do not provide lasting value. Other forms of bad debt include payday loans and any debt taken on to finance a lifestyle that exceeds one's income level. These types of debt can lead to financial strain and limit future opportunities, making it crucial to identify and avoid them when possible. Understanding the difference between good and bad debt empowers individuals to make informed financial decisions that can enhance their economic standing.

As you navigate your financial journey, remember to evaluate the purpose behind any debt you consider taking on. Always ask yourself if it will contribute positively to your financial future. Making deliberate choices about debt can greatly influence your overall financial health, paving the way for security and stability.

4.2 Strategies for Paying Off Debt

The Debt Snowball Method is a popular strategy that focuses on paying off your smallest debts first. This approach is rooted in the idea that achieving small victories can create a sense of momentum and motivate you to tackle larger debts. When you list your debts from smallest to largest, you start by putting all your extra money towards the smallest balance while making minimum payments on the others. Once that smallest debt is eliminated, you take the money you were using for that payment and apply it to the next smallest debt. This cycle continues as you knock out each balance one by one, like a snowball rolling down a hill growing larger with each payoff.

This method can be particularly effective for individuals who may feel overwhelmed by their debt loads. The psychological boost from quickly paying off smaller debts can build confidence and create positive financial habits. As you see your smaller balances disappear, you'll likely feel encouraged to continue the process. Remember, the key here is persistence and dedication to the plan. Tracking your progress can also heighten your motivation, allowing you to visualize how far you've come.

The Debt Avalanche Method, on the other hand, takes a more analytical approach by suggesting that you focus on paying off your highest-interest debts first. This method is designed to minimize the amount you pay in interest over time, ultimately leading to a faster overall payoff and less money spent. To implement this strategy, you begin by listing your debts from the highest interest rate to the lowest. Then, make minimum payments on all debts except for the one with the highest interest rate. Direct any extra funds toward that debt until it's gone.

4.3 The Role of Credit Scores in Financial Health

A credit score is a numerical representation of your creditworthiness, usually ranging from 300 to 850. This score is influenced by various factors, including your payment history, amount of debt, length of credit history, types of credit in use, and new credit inquiries. Payment history is the most significant factor, making up 35% of your score. Late payments or defaults can decrease your score dramatically. The amount of debt you owe accounts for 30% of your score; if you're using a large portion of your available credit, it can indicate risky behavior to lenders. Length of credit history impacts 15% of your score. Longer credit histories are generally favorable because they show a track record of managing credit responsibly. The types of credit you use, such as credit cards, mortgages, and auto loans, represent 10% of your score, while the remaining 10% relates to recent inquiries into your credit report.

Understanding your credit score is crucial because it plays a vital role in determining your eligibility for loans and credit cards. A higher credit score can lead to more favorable loan terms, lower interest rates, and even better insurance premiums. In many cases, lenders use your credit score to gauge how likely you are to repay borrowed funds. This means that if you plan to make a significant purchase, like a house or car, your credit score can significantly affect your financial future.

Improving your credit score is a practical goal that can lead to better financial opportunities. One of the most effective strategies is to pay your bills on time. Setting up automatic payments or reminders can help ensure you never miss a due date. Additionally, if you have existing debt, try to reduce it. Focus on paying down high-interest debts first while making at least the minimum payments on other accounts. Keeping your credit utilization ratio low is also important. Aim to use no more than 30% of your available credit limit, as high utilization can negatively impact your score.

Regularly reviewing your credit report is another beneficial practice. You can check your credit report for errors or discrepancies that could be hurting your score. If you find any mistakes, disputing them promptly can help improve your credit standing. Moreover, consider diversifying your credit by responsibly using different types of credit, like a mix of credit cards, personal loans, or installment loans. Each small positive change can contribute to boosting your score over time. Remember that rebuilding credit is a gradual process, so be patient and consistent in your efforts. Staying disciplined and informed will help you create a solid financial foundation for your future.

One useful tip for keeping your credit score healthy is to always keep an eye on your credit limit. If your lender increases your limit, resist the urge to spend up to that new limit. Instead, maintain your spending habits, as this can help keep your credit utilization low and, in turn, support a stronger credit score.

5. Saving Strategies

5.1 Building an Emergency Fund

An emergency fund is crucial for maintaining financial stability amidst life's uncertainties. Unexpected expenses can arise at any moment, whether it's a sudden medical emergency, car repairs, or unexpected unemployment. Without a financial safety net, these situations can lead to significant stress and potential debt. An emergency fund acts as a buffer, allowing individuals to navigate these challenges without derailing their financial goals. It can provide peace of mind and the confidence to handle life's surprises, knowing that you have resources set aside specifically for these situations. Having this fund can prevent you from resorting to credit cards or high-interest loans, which can add to your financial burden.

Determining how much to save can be a bit tricky, but a good rule of thumb is to aim for three to six months' worth of living expenses. This amount can cover your essential bills, such as your mortgage or rent, utilities, food, and transportation, in the event that your income ceases suddenly. Calculate your monthly expenses and multiply that number to find your ideal emergency fund target. However, the final amount may also depend on your personal circumstances, such as job security, health considerations, and dependents. If you work in a stable job with few financial obligations, three months' worth may suffice. Conversely, if you're self-employed or work in an unstable industry, consider leaning toward that six-month guideline. Assess your needs and lifestyle to find the right balance for you.

Starting your emergency fund doesn't have to be overwhelming. Begin with setting aside a small, manageable amount each month and gradually increase it as your financial situation improves. Automating your savings can help make this process seamless—set up a direct deposit from your paycheck into a separate savings account designated for emergencies. This way, you won't be tempted to dip into these savings for non-emergencies. Furthermore, review your emergency fund goals regularly, especially after significant life changes such as a new job, marriage, or the birth of a child, to ensure you are on track and prepared for whatever life throws your way.

5.2 High-Interest Savings Accounts vs. Regular Accounts

High-interest savings accounts can be a valuable tool for individuals looking to grow their money more effectively. Unlike regular savings accounts that typically offer lower interest rates, high-interest options provide better returns on your savings. This means that for every dollar you deposit, you can earn significantly more over time. The compounding effect of these higher interest rates can lead to substantial gains, especially if you keep your money in the account for an extended period. Moreover, many high-interest savings accounts have low or no fees associated with them, making them accessible without the worry of eroding your savings due to charges. Having your funds in a high-interest account not only helps you earn more, but it also encourages a disciplined savings habit, as the prospect of earning more can motivate individuals to save regularly.

When comparing account types, it's essential to evaluate factors such as interest rates, fees, accessibility, and the minimum balance requirements. Not all savings accounts are created equally, and understanding the differences can lead to better financial decisions. High-interest savings accounts usually come with higher interest rates than traditional savings accounts, which incentivizes account holders to keep their money deposited for longer. On the other hand, some regular accounts may have features like easier accessibility or overdraft protection that appeal to different needs. It's also important to factor in whether your account will be insured by the FDIC or NCUA. Finding the right balance between earning potential and convenience will ultimately help optimize your savings strategy and enhance your overall financial well-being.

As you explore high-interest savings accounts, consider setting up automatic transfers to this account from your checking account. Even small, regular contributions can significantly enhance your savings over time, especially when they are accruing higher interest. Additionally, regularly reviewing your account's interest rates and terms can help ensure that you are getting the best returns possible. Depending on market conditions, switching to a different account that offers a better rate may be necessary. Staying informed and proactive about your savings can make a big difference in reaching your financial goals.

5.3 Automating Your Savings

Automating your savings can be a game changer when it comes to achieving your financial goals. The primary benefit of automation is its ability to promote consistency. When you set up automatic transfers to your savings accounts, you're effectively treating savings like a regular bill that needs to be paid. This mindset shift helps ensure that money is set aside before you have a chance to spend it. Additionally, automation helps remove the temptation to spend money that should be saved, reducing the likelihood of impulsive purchases. This consistent contribution can lead to substantial growth over time, allowing you to reach milestones such as buying a home, going on a dream vacation, or building an emergency fund with ease.

Setting up automated transfers is a straightforward process. Start by identifying the amount of money you want to save each month. You can do this by reviewing your budget to find a comfortable figure that doesn't interfere with your essential expenses. Once you've determined the amount, access your bank's online banking platform or mobile app. Navigate to the transfer section and select your checking account as the source and a designated savings account as the destination. You'll typically find an option to make this transfer recurring, so choose a frequency that aligns with your pay schedule—monthly is a common choice. After entering the transfer details, confirm your settings, and you'll be all set. Remember to revisit this arrangement periodically; as your financial situation changes, you may find opportunities to increase your savings contributions.

To ensure your automated savings work effectively for you, consider setting specific savings goals. By having clear objectives, such as saving for a vacation or a car, you'll be more motivated to stick to your automated plan. Additionally, keep an eye on your savings goals and adjust your automated transfers as necessary. A good practice is to periodically reassess your budget and see if you can increase your savings amount whenever you get a raise or reduce your expenses. This proactive approach can enhance your financial stability and foster a healthy saving habit.

6. Understanding Investments

6.1 The Basics of Stocks, Bonds, and Mutual Funds

Stocks represent ownership in a company. When you buy a stock, you are purchasing a small piece of that company, which makes you a shareholder. This ownership means that you can potentially benefit from the company's success in the form of price appreciation and dividends. As a company's value increases, so does the price of its stock, and this can lead to significant financial gains. However, stock investments also carry risks; the price can fluctuate based on a variety of factors, including market conditions, economic trends, and company performance. Understanding how to analyze stocks and recognizing the importance of diversification can help in making informed decisions about where to invest your money.

Bonds are a different type of investment altogether. When you invest in bonds, you are lending money to a government, municipality, or corporation, in exchange for periodic interest payments and the return of the bond's face value at maturity. Bonds are considered fixed-income investments because they provide investors with a predictable income stream, which can help balance the higher volatility associated with stocks. They are generally seen as safer investments but typically offer lower potential returns than stocks. Mutual funds, on the other hand, are pools of money collected from multiple investors to invest in a diversified portfolio of stocks, bonds, or other securities. This allows individual investors to enjoy the benefits of diversification without needing to select each investment individually. By investing in mutual funds, you gain access to a range of assets and expertise that would otherwise be difficult to achieve on your own.

Both bonds and mutual funds can play essential roles in a well-rounded investment strategy. As you consider your financial goals, it may be helpful to think about your risk tolerance and how these different types of investments fit into your overall plan. Diversifying your portfolio by including a mix of stocks, bonds, and mutual funds can stabilize your potential returns while managing risk. For those looking to improve their personal finance, understanding these investment vehicles is crucial. A practical tip to remember is to review your financial situation regularly and adjust your investment strategy to meet your changing goals and the market landscape.

6.2 Investment Risks and Rewards

Investment risks manifest in various forms, depending on the type of investment. For example, stocks are susceptible to market volatility, meaning that their value can fluctuate wildly in short periods. Economic changes, such as recessions or shifts in consumer behavior, can heavily impact stock prices. Bonds, while generally viewed as safer, also carry risks. They can be affected by interest rate changes; as rates rise, existing bonds lose value in comparison to newly issued bonds with higher returns. Real estate investments come with their own set of risks, including property damage, market downturns, and location desirability fluctuations. Additionally, alternative investments like commodities or cryptocurrencies can be extremely volatile, further emphasizing the importance of understanding and assessing the level of risk before diving in.

The correlation between risk and reward is a fundamental principle in the world of investing. Generally, as the potential for reward increases, so does the risk involved. For instance, investing in start-ups can yield substantial returns if the company becomes successful, but the vast majority of new businesses fail, making this a high-risk arena. In contrast, investing in a stable blue-chip company may offer lower returns, but it typically comes with decreased risk, as these companies have established themselves over time. A balanced portfolio often reflects this relationship, incorporating diverse assets to mitigate risk while seeking potential rewards. Understanding that higher rewards usually come with increased risks can guide investors in making thoughtful, informed decisions.

One practical approach to managing investment risk is to diversify your portfolio. By spreading your investments across various asset classes, sectors, and geographical regions, you can reduce the impact of a poor-performing investment on your overall portfolio. Along with diversification, regularly reviewing and adjusting your investment strategy in response to market changes and personal financial goals is critical. Understanding your risk tolerance, or how much risk you are willing to take on, can significantly impact your investment decisions and help you align your strategy with your financial objectives.

6.3 How to Start Investing as a Beginner

Getting started with investing can seem daunting, especially if you have minimal experience. The first step is to educate yourself about the different investment options available. These include stocks, bonds, mutual funds, and real estate. Understanding the basics will help you make informed decisions. Start by setting clear financial goals. Consider what you want to achieve with your investments, whether itâ€™s saving for retirement, a home, or simply building wealth. Next, create a budget that allows you to set aside money for investing. An emergency fund should always be a priority, so ensure you have savings in place before you start investing. Once you're ready, you can open a brokerage account, which serves as your gateway to the investment world. Many platforms today offer user-friendly interfaces and resources tailored for beginners. It is also wise to start small; invest amounts that feel comfortable to you, and gradually increase your investment as you gain confidence. Regularly review your portfolio and stay informed about market trends, as this can help you make better investment choices in the future.

Building a diversified portfolio is crucial for minimizing investment risks. Put simply, diversification means spreading your investments across various asset classes and sectors. This strategy helps protect your portfolio from significant losses when one area of the market underperforms. For example, if you invest solely in technology stocks and that sector crashes, your entire portfolio could suffer. Instead, consider allocating funds not just to stocks but also to bonds and alternative investments like real estate or commodities. You can even diversify within asset classes; for instance, invest in different companies across various industries. Index funds and exchange-traded funds (ETFs) are excellent tools for beginners looking to diversify without having to pick individual stocks. They allow you to invest in a mix of assets efficiently and at a lower cost. By regularly rebalancing your portfolio, you can maintain your desired level of risk and ensure that no single investment becomes too dominant in your financial strategy. This careful planning can provide you with a smoother investing experience and steady growth over time.

A practical tip as you begin your investment journey is to keep a long-term perspective. Avoid the temptation to react to short-term market fluctuations, as these can lead to impulsive decisions that may hurt your financial goals. Focus on your strategic plan and make adjustments only when necessary, keeping an eye on your overall financial picture. Remember, investing is a marathon, not a sprint. Patience and discipline often yield the best results.

7. Retirement Planning

7.1 Why Start Early with Retirement Savings

Starting your retirement savings early is one of the smartest financial moves you can make. The magic of compound interest plays a pivotal role in this strategy. When you begin saving at a younger age, you not only invest your money but also give it time to grow exponentially. Compound interest works by calculating interest on your initial principal as well as the accumulated interest from previous periods. So, the earlier you start, the more time your money has to grow. For example, if you invest $5,000 a year starting at age 25 and continue until you are 35, you will accumulate a substantial amount by retirement age if you allow it to continue compounding. Waiting just a decade longer can significantly diminish the amount you would have at retirement. Therefore, even small contributions can lead to impressive results over time, thanks to this powerful financial principle.

Another key advantage of starting your retirement savings early is achieving long-term financial security. Investing as soon as possible means that you can weather market fluctuations and economic changes more effectively. Younger savers often have the luxury of time on their side, allowing them to ride out any downturns in the market. This ability to endure short-term volatility means your investments can recover and flourish over the long term. A worry-free retirement is achievable for those who prioritize early savings. Knowing that you have set aside a significant amount for your future allows you to enjoy life with less financial stress as you age. You will be positioned to make choices that enhance your quality of life in retirement, whether it means traveling, pursuing hobbies, or simply enjoying a comfortable lifestyle.

To maximize your retirement savings, consider taking advantage of employer-sponsored retirement plans if they are available to you. Many employers match contributions to retirement accounts, which effectively provides free money toward your savings. Additionally, think about setting up automatic contributions to your retirement accounts to ensure consistency and discipline in your saving habits. This way, you make saving a priority without having to remember to do it manually. The earlier you start and the more disciplined you are, the more prepared you will be for the future.

7.2 Types of Retirement Accounts Explained

401(k)s and Individual Retirement Accounts (IRAs) are two major types of retirement accounts that serve different roles in helping you save for your future. A 401(k) is typically offered by your employer and allows you to contribute a portion of your paycheck on a pre-tax basis, which can reduce your taxable income for the year. Many employers also match contributions up to a certain percentage, which means they effectively give you free money towards your retirement savings. On the other hand, an IRA is an individual account you can open on your own, independent of your employer. This gives you more control over your investments but does not come with matching contributions.

When it comes to choosing between these options, consider your employment situation and your retirement goals. If your employer offers a 401(k) with a matching contribution, it often makes sense to take advantage of that before contributing to an IRA. This is especially true if you're just starting your career and have limited funds to put aside. However, IRAs can be appealing because they offer more investment choices and flexibility compared to most 401(k) plans. Additionally, with a Traditional IRA, you can also take advantage of tax deductions, similar to a 401(k).

Both 401(k)s and IRAs come with specific contribution limits and tax implications that influence how much you can save and when you can access your funds. For 2023, the maximum contribution to a 401(k) is $22,500, or $30,000 if you are age 50 or older, thanks to a catch-up contribution. In contrast, the contribution limit for a Traditional or Roth IRA is $6,500, with an additional $1,000 for those aged 50 and up. Knowing these limits can help you strategically plan your contributions each year and maximize your savings.

Tax implications also vary significantly between these accounts. 401(k) contributions are made before taxes, meaning you'll pay taxes on withdrawals during retirement. Roth IRAs, however, use after-tax dollars, allowing your investments to grow tax-free, and withdrawals in retirement are typically tax-free as well. This makes Roth IRAs an attractive option for younger savers who expect to be in a higher tax bracket later in life. Furthermore, while 401(k) plans have specific withdrawal rules, which include penalties for early withdrawal before age 59½, IRAs can offer more flexibility. However, it's important to note that with both account types, early withdrawal may lead to taxes and penalties, so understanding the withdrawal rules is essential for financial planning.

To enhance your retirement planning, consider regularly reviewing your contributions and investment choices in both your 401(k) and IRA. Adjusting your strategy as your income grows or your financial circumstances change can make a significant difference in your retirement savings over time.

7.3 Calculating Your Retirement Needs

Estimating your future expenses is a crucial first step in planning for retirement. To project your retirement costs accurately, start by examining your current lifestyle. Consider all aspects of your daily life, such as housing, groceries, healthcare, transportation, and leisure activities. Think about how these costs might change in retirement. For instance, while some expenses, like commuting costs, may decrease, others, such as healthcare, typically rise as you age. A good approach is to create a detailed budget based on your current spending, adjusting for expected changes. Don't forget to account for inflation, which can erode your purchasing power over time. A common rule of thumb is to estimate that you will need around 70% to 80% of your pre-retirement income annually during retirement. However, everyone's situation is unique, so tailor your estimates to reflect your plans and lifestyle choices.

Once you have a good grasp of your expected expenses, the next step is to determine your savings goals. You need a strategy that will enable you to save enough to cover your projected expenses throughout retirement. Start by calculating how much money you will need saved by the time you retire. To do this, take your estimated annual expenses and multiply them by the number of years you anticipate being in retirement. For example, if your annual expenses are projected to be $50,000 and you expect to retire for 30 years, you will need around $1.5 million saved, assuming no other income sources. To achieve this goal, assess your current savings and develop a plan to increase contributions. Consider utilizing tax-advantaged accounts like IRAs or employer-sponsored 401(k)s, as these can significantly boost your savings through tax benefits and potential employer matches.

Keep in mind that regular reviews and adjustments to your plan are essential. Life circumstances, market fluctuations, and lifestyle choices can all impact your retirement needs. Make it a habit to evaluate your financial strategy annually, adjusting your savings rate, investment choices, or retirement date as necessary. Staying proactive will help ensure that you maintain a clear path toward your retirement goals, allowing for a comfortable and secure future. One practical tip is to automate your savings as much as possible. Setting up automatic transfers to your retirement accounts can help you stay disciplined and consistently work toward building your retirement nest egg without having to think about it.

8. Insurance and Protection

8.1 Types of Insurance You Need

Understanding the essential types of insurance is crucial for financial stability. Health insurance is perhaps the most important type, providing protection against high medical costs and access to necessary healthcare services. Whether you're visiting a doctor, undergoing surgery, or facing unexpected emergencies, having health insurance helps to ease financial burdens. Auto insurance is another key piece of the puzzle, safeguarding you from the risks associated with driving. It covers damage to your vehicle and liabilities in case of accidents, making it invaluable for protecting your assets and ensuring you're not left with overwhelming expenses from an unforeseen event. Home insurance protects your property and possessions, covering risks like theft, fire, or natural disasters. This not only offers peace of mind but also creates a safety net for your investment, helping you recover financially if something goes wrong.

Life and disability insurance are two other crucial types you should prioritize. Life insurance is designed to support your loved ones in the event of your untimely death. It provides a financial cushion at a time when they may be dealing with emotional distress and the sudden loss of income. This type of coverage can help them pay for daily living expenses, school tuition, and outstanding debts, ensuring their financial security. On the other hand, disability insurance is vital for protecting your earning potential. If you become unable to work due to illness or injury, this insurance replaces a portion of your income, allowing you to maintain your lifestyle and meet financial commitments. Having both life and disability insurance in place can significantly enhance your family's security, allowing you to focus on recovery and healing instead of worrying about money.

When it comes to managing your personal finances, itâ€™s beneficial to conduct regular reviews of your insurance policies to make sure they still meet your needs as your life changes. Life events such as marriage, having children, or changing jobs often necessitate adjustments to your coverage. Being proactive about your insurance means you can continue to protect yourself and your loved ones effectively. Look for opportunities to bundle policies, which can often save money, and always shop around to compare prices and coverage options. Prioritizing insurance is a smart step towards achieving and maintaining financial stability.

8.2 Assessing Your Insurance Needs

Evaluating your individual insurance needs is an important step in securing your financial future. To start, you should analyze your lifestyle, assets, and responsibilities. Consider what you own, such as your home, car, and personal belongings, as these are the primary assets you want to protect. Next, think about your lifestyle. Do you have a family that depends on your income? Do you have significant debts like a mortgage or student loans? These factors will guide you in determining the coverage you require. For instance, if you have a family, life insurance might be crucial to ensure their well-being in case of an unexpected emergency. Additionally, consider any health issues or unique circumstances that may require specialized coverage, such as long-term care insurance. By thoroughly examining these aspects, you can better understand the types and amounts of insurance you need.

Life is ever-changing, and so are your insurance needs. It's essential to revisit your insurance policies regularly, particularly after significant life events such as marriage, the birth of a child, or a new job. Each of these milestones can alter your financial responsibilities and what coverage is appropriate. When adjusting your coverage, think about increases in income that may affect your lifestyle or the need for additional liability protection if you start a business. You should also examine your existing policies to see if they still align with your current situation. For example, if your children have grown up and moved out, you might no longer need as much life insurance. Make it a habit to review your insurance policies at least once a year, or better yet, after any major life changes, to ensure that you are neither underinsured nor overpaying for coverage you no longer need.

Understanding your insurance needs is not just about choosing the right policies but also about knowing when to make changes. Keep an organized file of all your insurance documents, including your policy details, and make notes on when the next review should take place. Additionally, consider speaking with an insurance advisor or financial planner who can offer personalized recommendations based on your specific circumstances. This proactive approach will not only provide you with peace of mind but can also lead to savings in premiums while ensuring that your coverage aligns with your life's current reality.

8.3 Understanding Deductibles and Premiums

Insurance premiums are the amounts you pay to maintain your insurance coverage. This payment can be made monthly, quarterly, or annually, depending on the terms of your policy. Premiums are essentially the cost of having insurance, and they can vary significantly based on multiple factors, including the type of coverage, your location, your age, and even your credit score. Understanding your premiums is crucial because they can greatly impact your overall financial situation. When budgeting, it's important to remember that while you want adequate coverage, higher premiums can strain your finances, particularly if you stretch your budget to secure a plan that offers better coverage than what you actually need. Analyzing your insurance needs carefully can help you determine the right balance between what you can spend and the level of protection you genuinely require.

Deductibles play a significant role in your total insurance costs and are essentially the amount you must pay out-of-pocket before your insurance coverage starts to kick in. For example, if you have a deductible of $1,000 on your homeowners insurance, you will need to pay this amount for any claim before your insurance provider pays the remainder. Typically, plans with lower premiums come with higher deductibles, and conversely, plans with higher premiums usually have lower deductibles. This can create a tricky balancing act when selecting coverage. It's wise to consider your financial situation—if you can comfortably manage the deductible during an unexpected event, opting for a lower premium may save you money in the long run. Understanding how various deductible options affect your premiums can empower you to make more informed choices in your insurance shopping process.

To maximize your insurance strategy, regularly review your premiums and deductibles as part of your overall financial planning. As your life changes—be it through marriage, having children, or changes in asset value—reassessing your insurance needs can uncover significant savings. Additionally, consider bundling policies, such as auto and homeowner's insurance, to benefit from potential discounts. By staying informed and proactive about your insurance coverage, you can protect your financial health more effectively.

9. Tax Planning Basics

9.1 Understanding Your Tax Bracket

A tax bracket is essentially a range of income levels that determines the rate at which your income is taxed. In many countries, including the United States, tax systems are progressive, meaning that as you earn more money, you pay a higher percentage on the income that falls within specific ranges. Each bracket has its own tax rate. This means that if you're earning a salary or other income, only the portion of your income that falls within a specific bracket is taxed at that bracket's rate. For instance, if your income places you in the 22% tax bracket, you won't pay 22% on all your income, just on the amount that exceeds the higher threshold of your previous bracket. Understanding how tax brackets work helps you anticipate your tax obligations and informs your financial planning.

Calculating your tax obligation involves knowing your estimated taxable income and which tax brackets apply to you. Start by calculating your total income for the year and then subtract any deductions you qualify for. These deductions reduce your taxable income, allowing you to pay less in taxes overall. Once you have your estimated taxable income, you can apply the current tax rates to each portion of your income falling within the different brackets. For example, if your taxable income is $50,000 and the first $10,000 is taxed at 10%, the next $30,000 is taxed at 12%, and the final $10,000 at 22%, you'll need to calculate how much you owe at each rate. This method provides a clearer picture of your financial liability while allowing you to plan more effectively for payments due, potential refunds, or any necessary adjustments throughout the year.

It's crucial to stay informed about changes in tax laws and brackets, as these can affect your financial strategies. Each year, the IRS updates these brackets, so keeping an eye on any adjustments may help you plan better. Use tax planning software or consult a tax professional to aid in accurate calculations and to make sure you're taking advantage of all possible deductions. Additionally, maintaining organized records of your income and expenses can significantly simplify the tax filing process. By understanding your tax bracket and calculating your obligations accurately, you can make more informed decisions about your finances and potentially save money in tax payments.

9.2 Deductions and Credits You Should Know

Understanding deductions is crucial for anyone looking to optimize their tax situation and lower their taxable income. Deductions are various expenses that the tax code allows you to subtract from your total income, effectively reducing the amount of income that is subject to taxation. One common type of deduction is the standard deduction, which for many filers simplifies the process by providing a fixed amount that reduces the income on which taxes are calculated. However, if you have significant expenses that qualify, itemizing your deductions may yield greater tax savings. Common itemizable expenses include mortgage interest, medical expenses exceeding a certain percentage of your adjusted gross income, and charitable contributions. It's essential to keep detailed records of these expenses throughout the year to ensure you can take full advantage of every deduction available to you.

Knowing tax credits is also an important part of tax planning. Unlike deductions, which reduce your taxable income, tax credits directly reduce the amount of tax you owe, making them potentially more valuable. For instance, if you owe $1,000 in taxes and qualify for a $200 tax credit, your tax liability is reduced to $800. There are various credits available, including those for education expenses, energy efficiency improvements in your home, and those specifically for families, such as the Child Tax Credit. Understanding the difference between deductions and credits can empower you to make strategic decisions about your finances. While both are beneficial, focusing on credits can often lead to more immediate savings on your tax bill.

Being aware of special credits and deductions tailored to your unique situation can make a significant impact on your finances. For instance, if you are a first-time homebuyer, there may be specific deductions or credits available to help lighten your financial load. Additionally, if you are self-employed, you can deduct certain business expenses that others cannot. It's also worthwhile to explore any state-specific tax credits or deductions that might be available in your area. Always keep informed about any changes in tax laws as they can open new opportunities for savings. As a practical tip, set aside time each year to review your financial situation and adjust your tax strategy accordingly to ensure you're maximizing available deductions and credits.

9.3 Tax-Advantaged Accounts and Their Benefits

Tax-advantaged accounts are specific types of financial accounts designed to help individuals save money while reducing their tax burdens. These accounts include Individual Retirement Accounts (IRAs) and Health Savings Accounts (HSAs), both of which provide unique tax benefits. With IRAs, contributions may be tax-deductible, which means that you can lower your taxable income for the year you contribute. This setup allows your money to grow tax-deferred until you withdraw it in retirement, often when your tax rate may be lower. HSAs function similarly for healthcare expenses; they allow you to set aside pre-tax dollars to cover qualified medical costs. The money contributed to an HSA is tax-deductible, reducing your taxable income, and when used for qualified expenses, distributions are tax-free, making it a powerful tool for managing healthcare costs.

Maximizing the benefits of tax-advantaged accounts requires strategic planning. First, you should understand the contribution limits and eligibility requirements for each account. For instance, it's crucial to contribute the maximum allowable amount to your IRA or HSA each year to take full advantage of these tax benefits. Utilizing automatic contributions can ensure that you consistently add to these accounts without needing to think about it. Another effective strategy is to prioritize using an HSA for your healthcare expenses, as it not only offers tax-free withdrawals but can also serve as an additional retirement savings tool if you do not need to use it for current medical costs. This dual-use aspect of HSAs can significantly enhance your overall financial strategy.

Moreover, consider the long-term impact of your contributions and the compounding interest they can generate. Any growth in your investments within an IRA or HSA is tax-deferred, meaning your money can work harder for you without immediate tax consequences. This makes beginning your contributions as early as possible a wise choice. Be sure to invest wisely within these accounts, focusing on a diversified mix of assets that align with your risk tolerance and financial goals. Staying informed about your account's rules and periodically reviewing your contributions and investment strategies will help you maximize the benefits of tax-advantaged accounts. Remember to keep receipts for any qualified expenses to fully leverage the tax-free distributions from your HSA—this service is the cherry on top of its already favorable tax treatment.

10. Financial Tools and Apps

10.1 Best Budgeting Apps for Personal Finance

Many people today find themselves relying on budgeting apps to help manage their finances effectively. These apps are designed to streamline the budgeting process, making it easier to track spending, set financial goals, and plan for the future, ultimately leading to better money management. Popular options like Mint, YNAB (You Need a Budget), and PocketGuard serve a wide range of users, from novices just starting out to more experienced budgeters looking for advanced features. Mint offers a comprehensive overview of all your finances, linking bank accounts and credit cards to show a complete picture of your spending and saving. YNAB, on the other hand, emphasizes proactive budgeting, encouraging users to give every dollar a job and adapt their budgets continually. PocketGuard simplifies the process by showing how much disposable income you have after accounting for bills, goals, and necessities, making it great for quick financial checks. Each of these applications has garnered a loyal following by addressing various expenses and usage scenarios, appealing to different financial habits and objectives.

When selecting a budgeting app, look for key features that suit your individual needs. User interface plays a significant role; an app that is easy to navigate will make it more likely that you will stick with your budgeting efforts. A clear layout helps users quickly input expenses and understand their financial status at a glance. Security is another crucial consideration, especially when apps request access to bank accounts. Ensure the app uses encryption and follows best practices for data safety to keep your information secure. Flexibility is also important; applications that allow you to customize categories for expenses, set different types of budgets, and adjust goals can help you tailor your financial strategy. Integration with other financial tools, like investment accounts, can be beneficial for those looking to manage their full financial picture in one place. Notifications and reminders can assist in staying on track with bills and budget limits, which helps cultivate healthy spending habits.

Understanding your personal finance needs can guide you towards the app that works best for you. Take the time to evaluate what you want out of a budgeting app—whether it's ease of use, detailed reporting, or stringent financial controls—and consider trying out a few options, as many offer free trials. Remember that the best app is the one that aligns with your financial goals and motivates you to stay engaged with your budgeting journey. Finding an app that fits seamlessly into your lifestyle can make a significant difference in managing your finances successfully.

10.2 Using Spreadsheets for Budgeting

Creating a personalized budgeting spreadsheet can significantly simplify the way you manage your finances. Begin by opening a spreadsheet application like Microsoft Excel or Google

Sheets. Start by labeling the first row with headers that are essential for tracking your income and expenses. Common headers might include Date, Description, Category, Amount, and Notes. Once you have your headers in place, allocate sections for both your income and expenses. For income, list all your sources, such as salary, freelance work, or any side business. On the expense side, categorize your spending such as housing, utilities, groceries, transportation, entertainment, and savings. This will help you visualize where your money is going. As you input your data, make sure to update it regularly, ideally on a weekly basis, to maintain an accurate reflection of your financial situation. You might also consider color-coding categories to make it visually appealing and easier to analyze at a glance.

Utilizing spreadsheet functions can elevate the accuracy of your budgeting efforts, making it easier to calculate totals and track your progress. Basic functions like SUM are essential for adding up your income and expenses, while using simple formulas, such as subtracting total expenses from total income, can quickly show you your net savings or deficit. For even greater detail, employ conditional formatting to automatically highlight areas where you're overspending in a specific category, so you can make adjustments. Functions like AVERAGE can be helpful for gauging your typical spending in each category over time. If you're planning for future expenses, consider using the IF function for expected scenarios; for example, you can set a threshold that alerts you when an expense exceeds a budgeted amount. Embracing these functions not only streamlines your budgeting process but also makes it more insightful, offering clarity on your financial habits and helping you make informed decisions moving forward.

Setting aside a few hours every month to review and adjust your budget will empower you to stay aligned with your financial goals, creating a clear path toward better money management.

10.3 Online Tools for Tracking Investments

Investment tracking tools have become essential for anyone looking to keep a close eye on their financial growth. Various online platforms, such as personal finance apps and investment trackers, allow users to monitor the performance of their portfolios in real-time. These tools often come with features that provide insights into your investments, such as visual graphs, performance trends, and detailed reports. Popular platforms like Mint, Personal Capital, and Robinhood not only help you see the current value of your assets but also allow you to categorize your investments, set goals, and receive alerts about market changes. By utilizing these online tools, investors can simplify the often complex task of managing their finances and remain informed to make better investment decisions.

Analyzing investment performance is crucial for anyone who wants to ensure their portfolio is on track for growth. Most investment tracking tools provide various metrics that help assess the health of your investments. Many allow users to evaluate returns over different periods, compare current performance against benchmarks, and examine asset allocation. By conducting regular check-ups on your investments, you can identify which assets may be underperforming and adjust your strategy accordingly. Moreover, some platforms offer predictive analytics, enabling investors to forecast potential performance based on historical data. Utilizing these insights not only enhances your understanding of market dynamics but also empowers you to refine your investment approach, ensuring a better alignment with your financial goals.

To maximize the benefits of these online tools, consider integrating multiple platforms to gain diverse perspectives on your investment performance. Each tool may offer unique features or insights that can complement one another, leading to a more comprehensive view of your financial situation. Additionally, take the time to regularly update and customize your tracking settings, such as performance benchmarks or risk tolerance levels, to keep your assessment relevant. Engaging with these tools not only provides clarity but also fosters a more proactive approach to building and maintaining a robust investment portfolio.

11. Building Wealth Over Time

11.1 The Power of Compound Interest

Compound interest is a powerful tool in personal finance that allows your money to grow at an accelerated rate over time. Unlike simple interest, which is calculated only on the principal amount, compound interest is calculated on both the principal and the accumulated interest. This means that as your investment earns interest, that interest also begins to earn interest, leading to exponential growth. For example, if you invest $1,000 at an annual interest rate of 5%, you would earn $50 in the first year. However, in the second year, you'd earn interest not just on the original $1,000 but on $1,050, resulting in $52.50 in interest for that year. Over several years, this compounding effect can significantly increase the total amount in your account, transforming small investments into substantial sums.

Understanding the impact of time on compound interest is crucial. The earlier you start investing, the more time your money has to grow. Even a small amount can lead to impressive results if left to compound over years or decades. This is why itâ€™s commonly suggested that individuals begin saving for retirement as soon as possible. Tools like retirement accounts and mutual funds typically take advantage of compound interest, making them ideal for long-term savings. The 'time value of money' principle underscores that money available today is worth more than the same amount in the future due to its potential earning capability, primarily through compound interest.

To truly harness the power of compound interest, it's essential to adopt strategies that encourage reinvestment of earnings. One effective approach is to choose accounts or investment vehicles that offer high-interest rates or returns. High-yield savings accounts and interest-bearing investments can accumulate wealth more rapidly. Additionally, consider setting up automatic contributions to your investments. By consistently adding to your principal, you're not only increasing the amount of money that earns interest but also taking advantage of dollar-cost averaging.

Reinvesting dividends and interest payments is another strategy that can have a substantial impact. Instead of withdrawing earnings, reinvest them to purchase more shares or increase the principal. This creates a snowball effect, compounding your returns even further. Monitoring and adjusting your investment strategy can also help maximize your compound interest earnings. As your financial situation changes, reassess your investment choices to ensure they align with your long-term goals. By staying informed and proactive, you can optimize the benefits of compound interest, laying a strong foundation for financial growth.

Consider that even small increases in your contribution or return rate can significantly impact your wealth over time. For instance, increasing your monthly savings by just $50 can lead to tens of thousands more in retirement simply due to the effect of compounding. This highlights the importance of making financial decisions that leverage time and reinvestment, which ultimately pave the way to greater financial security.

11.2 Diversifying Your Investment Portfolio

Understanding the importance of diversification is crucial for anyone looking to grow their wealth while managing risk. By spreading investments across different asset classesâ€"such as stocks, bonds, real estate, and commoditiesâ€"investors can reduce the impact of a poor-performing investment on their overall portfolio. When one asset class suffers a downturn, others may remain stable or even appreciate, helping to cushion potential losses. Furthermore, diversification can enhance returns over time. By holding a mix of investments, investors often take advantage of various market conditions, maximizing their potential for profit. This strategy is not only about avoiding losses but also about positioning oneself to benefit from various economic cycles.

To effectively diversify your portfolio, one needs to take a few crucial steps. Start by analyzing your current investments, which might reveal concentrations in certain sectors or asset types. Then, look to balance these by incorporating different asset classes. Stocks can be paired with bonds for stability, while real estate can provide a hedge against inflation. Beyond asset classes, consider diversifying within sectors by investing in various industries like technology, healthcare, and consumer goods. Geographic diversification can also be valuable since markets around the world do not always move in sync. Investing in international funds or companies can capture growth in emerging markets, which may outperform domestic stocks at times.

As you look to diversify, remember that itâ€™s essential to keep your investment goals, risk tolerance, and time horizon in mind. A well-rounded approach tailored to your financial situation will yield more favorable outcomes. One practical tip is to periodically review your investment allocations and make adjustments based on market conditions or changes in your personal circumstances. By staying vigilant and flexible, you can effectively manage risk and seize opportunities as they arise, ensuring your portfolio remains robust and resilient.

11.3 Real Estate as an Investment Option

Investing in real estate can offer significant benefits, making it an attractive option for those looking to diversify their investment portfolios. One of the main advantages is the potential for passive income through rental properties. Owning a rental property can generate regular cash flow, providing a steady supplemental income that can help enhance your financial stability. Furthermore, real estate often appreciates over time, allowing you to build equity that can contribute to your net worth. Additionally, real estate investments can provide tax benefits, such as deductions on mortgage interest and property depreciation, which can further improve your overall financial situation.

However, it is essential to acknowledge the drawbacks of real estate investing. It requires a significant upfront investment, which can be a barrier for some individuals. Maintenance costs, property management, and the potential for vacancies can also eat into profits. Moreover, the real estate market can be volatile, influenced by economic downturns and shifts in demand. Effective research and planning are crucial to mitigate these risks and ensure that real estate fits seamlessly into your broader investment strategy.

There are various ways to invest in real estate, catering to different risk appetites and financial capabilities. Rental properties are one of the most traditional forms of real estate investment; they provide direct control and the possibility of long-term gains. Real Estate Investment Trusts (REITs) offer a more hands-off approach, allowing you to invest in real estate portfolios without having to buy and manage properties directly. This can be a good option for those who want to get into real estate but lack the time or resources to manage a physical property. Crowdfunding platforms have also emerged as a popular alternative, allowing multiple investors to pool resources for larger real estate projects. This can help you diversify your investments with relatively small amounts of capital, making real estate more accessible than ever before.

When considering which method to pursue, it's crucial to align your investment choice with your financial goals and risk tolerance. Each option has its unique set of risks and rewards, so appropriate research and careful selection can lead to successful outcomes. Staying informed and being adaptable to market changes can help you navigate the complexities of real estate investing. Always take into account not only the figures but also thorough due diligence to ensure that your chosen path aligns with your financial objectives.

12. Navigating Financial Crises

12.1 Creating a Financial Crisis Plan

Identifying potential financial crises is an essential first step in creating a financial crisis plan. A financial crisis can take various forms, such as job loss, medical emergencies, or unexpected major expenses. Understanding these possibilities is crucial because it empowers you to prepare in advance rather than reactively. Life is unpredictable, and financial hardships can arise from factors beyond your control. By anticipating these crises and recognizing the stress they can cause, you can appreciate the importance of having a solid financial plan in place. With a well-thought-out strategy, you can mitigate the impact of these challenges on your life and maintain a sense of control even in turbulent times.

Developing a contingency plan means creating a personalized financial strategy that addresses potential emergencies effectively. Start by examining your current financial situation, including income, expenses, savings, and debts. This analysis allows you to identify areas where you can cut back or save in advance. Consider setting aside an emergency fund that covers at least three to six months of living expenses. This fund will act as a safety net, providing you the financial protection you need when facing unexpected costs. Additionally, explore various insurance options, such as health, disability, or renters insurance, which can protect against significant financial burdens. Regularly review and update your plan, as your financial situation and life circumstances can change over time. Taking proactive steps today will help you feel more secure about tomorrow.

Creating a successful financial crisis plan involves understanding risks and taking practical steps to protect yourself and your finances. Monitor your progress and adapt your plan as necessary, ensuring it evolves with your life circumstances. Communicate openly with family members or partners about your plan so everyone is on the same page and can contribute to the effort. Consider using budgeting tools or financial software that can help simulate different scenarios, making it easier to identify weaknesses and develop actionable strategies. One practical tip is to automate your savings by setting up recurring transfers to your emergency fund or separate savings account. This way, you're consistently building your financial safety net without having to think about it. Being prepared is key to navigating the inevitable financial challenges life may throw your way.

12.2 Communicating About Money with Family

Discussing finances with family members plays a critical role in fostering healthy relationships and achieving financial well-being. Open financial dialogue can reduce misunderstandings, prevent conflict, and encourage a culture of transparency and trust. When family members talk about money matters, they can share their hopes, concerns, and expectations, allowing for informed decision-making regarding spending, saving, and investment. This communication is particularly vital in today's world, where financial pressure can create emotional stress. Being able to express thoughts and feelings about money can lead to better financial decisions and a sense of unity within the family, helping everyone to work towards common financial goals.

Creating an atmosphere conducive to financial discussions requires thoughtfulness and intentionality. Start by setting aside time for family meetings dedicated to finances, ensuring that everyone feels prepared to participate without distractions. It can be helpful to establish ground rules that promote respect and openness, allowing each member to express their views without judgment. Using questions to guide the conversation can also spark meaningful discussions. For instance, asking about financial dreams or discussing budget priorities can provide an engaging platform for sharing ideas. Be sure to represent all age groups in these discussions, as each person's perspective can offer valuable insights and lead to building collective strategies for better financial management.

In this journey of communicating about money, consider practicing active listening techniques. This means not only hearing what others are saying but also acknowledging their emotions and validating their concerns. When family members feel heard, they are more likely to engage positively in the conversation, making it easier to address financial issues collaboratively. A practical tip is to make the financial discussions regular, rather than only initiating them during crises or disagreements. Scheduling monthly or quarterly financial check-ins can normalize the conversation about money, making it less daunting and more routine. This habit can strengthen familial bonds and contribute to better financial literacy and collective responsibility.

12.3 Resources for Financial Assistance

Identifying financial assistance programs is an essential step for anyone facing financial hardships. There are numerous resources available through government agencies, non-profits, and local community organizations designed to help individuals during tough times. Federal programs such as Temporary Assistance for Needy Families (TANF) provide cash assistance to low-income families with children, while Supplemental Nutrition Assistance Program (SNAP) helps with food costs. Community resources like food banks, shelters, and clothing drives can offer immediate relief. Additionally, many states have their own specific programs tailored to assist residents in need. It's crucial to research local initiatives, as they may offer grants, low-interest loans, or utility assistance that are not well known but can significantly ease financial burden.

Reaching out for help is often a daunting task but is essential for obtaining the financial assistance needed. When seeking aid, it's important to be organized and prepared. Gather relevant documents such as income statements, tax returns, and proof of expenses to present a clear picture of your financial situation. Many organizations have specific application processes, so familiarize yourself with each program's requirements. Being transparent and honest about your circumstances will not only help you find the right resources but can also open doors to additional support options. Don't hesitate to communicate your needs; whether it's through phone calls, emails, or in-person visits, being proactive in seeking assistance can significantly increase your chances of receiving help.

Utilizing online resources can also enhance your ability to find and apply for financial assistance. Websites like Benefits.gov can help you discover what programs you may qualify for by simply answering a few questions about your situation. Local social service offices often have forums or hotlines where you can ask questions and get guidance. Remember that seeking help is a sign of strength, not weakness, and there are numerous people and organizations willing to support you. One practical tip is to keep a list of important contacts and deadlines, ensuring that you don't miss out on any potential assistance opportunities. In times of financial stress, being proactive and informed can make a substantial difference in your situation.

13. The Role of Financial Advisors

13.1 When to Consider Hiring a Financial Advisor

Understanding your financial landscape is essential, and there are clear indicators that suggest it might be time to consider hiring a financial advisor. If you find yourself facing complex financial decisions, like navigating investments, planning for retirement, or managing tax strategies, these might be signs that your current knowledge or time investment isn't sufficient. Major life changes such as marriage, divorce, the birth of a child, or a significant career shift can also trigger the need for professional guidance. These transitions often come with financial implications that can be overwhelming to manage alone.

Another important indicator is the feeling of being out of control or uncertain about your financial future. If you struggle to create a budget, often find yourself confused by financial jargon, or hesitate when it comes to making investment choices, reaching out for help can provide clarity. Additionally, if you have recently received an inheritance or come into a sudden windfall, an advisor can help you allocate your new resources wisely. Recognizing these signs early can set you on a path toward better financial health and peace of mind.

The advantages of working with a financial advisor are numerous and can significantly enhance your financial life. A professional can provide personalized advice tailored to your specific needs and goals, making complex financial matters feel more manageable. They have the expertise to analyze your current situation, identify potential pitfalls, and help you build a strategy that aligns with your aspirations, whether it's saving for a child's education, purchasing a home, or planning for retirement.

Moreover, a financial advisor serves as a valuable sounding board for your ideas and concerns, offering insights that you might not have considered. They can help you stay disciplined and focused on your long-term goals, especially during periods of market volatility or personal uncertainty. The peace of mind that comes from knowing professionals are helping you navigate financial decisions can be invaluable, allowing you to concentrate on other important aspects of your life. A practical tip for anyone considering a financial advisor is to look for someone who offers a free initial consultation. This can give you a sense of their approach and determine if they're the right fit for your needs.

13.2 Understanding Different Fee Structures

Understanding the different types of advisor fees is crucial when you seek financial guidance. There are two primary fee structures used by financial advisors: commission-based and fee-only. Commission-based advisors earn their income through commissions on the products they sell. This means their payment is tied to transactions, such as mutual funds or insurance policies. While this model might seem appealing because it often comes with low upfront costs, it can create a conflict of interest, as advisors could recommend products that yield higher commissions rather than what is best for you. Fee-only advisors, on the other hand, charge based on a flat fee, an hourly rate, or a percentage of your assets under management. This structure can align the advisor's interests more closely with yours because they receive payment regardless of which investments you choose, allowing for unbiased advice focused solely on your needs.

Choosing the right fee model is essential for your financial planning success. To determine which fee structure suits your needs, consider your financial situation, investment goals, and preferred level of ongoing support. If you prefer a straightforward relationship where you pay for services without worrying about hidden commissions, a fee-only advisor may be the best option. Conversely, if you are comfortable with a commission-based approach and are confident in evaluating the products and services being offered, this structure could work for you. Reflect on the complexity of your financial situation as well; if your finances are relatively straightforward, a simpler fee structure might suffice. However, for more complicated scenarios, a fee-only model may offer the depth of planning and tailored advice that you need.

Ultimately, regardless of the fee structure you choose, it's important to clearly understand all costs involved before committing to an advisor. Transparency is key in finance, and a good advisor will gladly provide a clear breakdown of their fees and how they affect your overall investment. Always ask questions and ensure you are comfortable with the terms before moving forward. Additionally, consider regularly reviewing your relationship with your advisor to ensure that their fee structure continues to meet your changing needs.

13.3 Questions to Ask a Potential Advisor

Before hiring a financial advisor, it's crucial to prepare for the interview by formulating questions that align with your financial goals. Start by asking about the advisor's qualifications and credentials. Understanding their education and certifications such as CFP, CFA, or CPA can provide insight into their expertise. Inquire about their experience in your specific financial needs, whether that includes retirement planning, tax strategies, or investment management. This helps ascertain whether they can meet your unique circumstances. Another essential question is about their investment philosophy. Knowing whether they lean towards active or passive investment strategies, and how they handle market volatility can influence your decision. Additionally, you should ask about their fee structure. Understanding how they charge—whether it's a flat fee, hourly rate, or a percentage of assets under management—will help you gauge how this fits into your budget. Asking about the services included in their fees can clarify what you're paying for. Communication style is equally important; you want an advisor whose frequency of communication and responsiveness aligns with your expectations. Don't overlook their approach to client education. A good advisor should educate you on financial matters, empowering you to make informed decisions alongside their guidance. This preparation can lead to a productive conversation that reveals whether they can be a good financial partner for you.

As you listen to an advisor's responses, it's important to evaluate the clarity and confidence of their answers. Look for advisors who provide comprehensive responses without jargon, ensuring you fully understand their concepts. Their ability to explain complex ideas in simple terms shows not only their knowledge but also their willingness to help you grasp essential financial details. Pay attention to how they address your specific questions. A fitting advisor should take the time to provide tailored answers rather than offering generic solutions. Consider their examples: practical illustrations of how they have helped clients in the past can shed light on their capabilities. Assess their honesty and transparency. If an advisor is evasive or unwilling to share relevant details about their fees or investment performance, it may indicate a lack of integrity. Additionally, their enthusiasm for your financial well-being can be a positive sign. An advisor who shows genuine interest in your goals and engages in a two-way dialogue demonstrates a commitment to your financial success. Finally, trust your instincts. If something feels off or if you feel pressured during the conversation, consider it a red flag. It's essential to work with someone who listens, respects your input, and fosters a healthy advisor-client relationship.

When dealing with potential financial advisors, remember that this process is about finding the right fit for you. Take your time, and don't hesitate to meet with multiple advisors before making a decision. Trust your intuition, amidst the facts and figures, to choose an advisor who resonates with your financial values and objectives.

14. Financial Independence and Early Retirement (FIRE)

14.1 Key Concepts Behind FIRE

The FIRE movement, which stands for Financial Independence, Retire Early, is centered on the idea of achieving financial freedom at a young age, allowing individuals to retire much earlier than the traditional retirement age. The core principles of FIRE revolve around aggressive saving, strategic budgeting, and smart investing. Advocates often recommend saving 50% or more of one's income, which can be achieved by significantly cutting back on expenses. This means assessing every aspect of spending, from housing and transportation to leisure activities, and finding areas to reduce costs. By maximizing savings, participants can invest their surplus in various assets, such as stocks or real estate, that ideally provide a return substantial enough to support their lifestyle in retirement.

Despite its growing popularity, the FIRE approach is often misunderstood. Many mistakenly believe that those who follow the FIRE path live a life of deprivation, constantly sacrificing joy in the present for an uncertain future. In reality, the movement encourages a deliberate and mindful approach to spending. While sacrifices may be necessary, practitioners learn to redirect their finances toward what truly matters to them, allowing them to enjoy a fulfilling life now, while still planning for the future. Another common misconception is that FIRE is for the wealthy. However, the principles of FIRE can be applied by people of various economic backgrounds. Success in the FIRE movement relies more on discipline and awareness of personal finance than on a high income.

To effectively adopt the FIRE lifestyle, it's essential to focus not only on saving and investing but also on cultivating a mindset of financial literacy. Understanding concepts like compound interest, asset allocation, and the importance of passive income can empower individuals to make informed financial decisions. A practical tip for anyone interested in FIRE is to start tracking your expenses. Use an app or a simple spreadsheet to see where your money goes each month. This awareness can unveil patterns in spending behavior you may not have noticed before and can lead to meaningful changes that accelerate your journey toward financial independence.

14.2 Strategies for Achieving Financial Independence

Developing a savings plan is essential if you want to achieve financial independence and retire early, commonly known as the FIRE movement. The first step in creating an effective savings strategy is to set clear and realistic goals. Start by determining how much money you will need to live comfortably without a regular paycheck. This requires some research into your expected expenses in retirement, taking into account housing, healthcare, lifestyle, and any potential taxes. Once you have a target number, you can reverse-engineer your savings plan. Consider cutting out unnecessary expenses. This doesn't mean a total lifestyle overhaul but rather identifying areas where you can trim the excess without sacrificing your happiness. Many find that by examining subscriptions, dining out habits, or other discretionary spending, they can free up a significant portion of their income for savings.

Another effective tactic is to automate your savings. By setting up automatic transfers into a savings account or investment account, you ensure that saving becomes a priority. Treating savings like a mandatory expense helps you build your nest egg without second-guessing or having to think about it every month. Additionally, consider taking advantage of tax-advantaged accounts like IRAs or 401(k)s, which allow your money to grow tax-free or tax-deferred. This can be a powerful tool in your savings strategy, allowing you to accumulate wealth faster than in a standard savings account. Lastly, aim for a savings rate of at least 50% of your income if possible. This aggressive approach might require drastic changes initially, but it can set you on a direct path toward financial independence much quicker.

Investing wisely is crucial in your journey toward financial independence. While saving is essential, simply accumulating cash in a savings account may not yield the desired results over time due to inflation eroding its value. Begin by educating yourself about different investment vehicles. Stocks, bonds, mutual funds, and exchange-traded funds (ETFs) are popular options worth considering. Stocks, while more volatile, have the potential for high returns over the long haul. Considering a diversified portfolio can help mitigate risk while still allowing for growth. Learning about index funds can also be beneficial; these funds track market indices and often have lower fees compared to actively managed funds, making them a cost-effective option.

Real estate is another avenue that can significantly accelerate your path to financial independence. Owning rental properties can generate passive income and provide tax benefits. Alternatively, real estate investment trusts (REITs) offer a way to invest in real estate without the hassles of managing properties directly. Beyond traditional investments, explore alternatives like peer-to-peer lending or investing in your own business as ways to grow your wealth. Always remember the importance of having a solid emergency fund, ideally covering three to six months of living expenses, before diving more deeply into investments. This grounding can help you withstand any market fluctuations without derailing your financial goals. Start experimenting with small amounts, develop a strategy that reflects your risk tolerance, and consistently evaluate your portfolio to navigate your financial journey efficiently.

As you progress, keep in mind the importance of continual learning and adapting your strategies based on your experiences and changing financial landscape. In personal finance, discipline, and informed decision-making will pave the way toward your financial independence.

14.3 Potential Challenges and How to Overcome Them

Many people pursuing financial independence face common obstacles that can derail their plans if not addressed. One major challenge is the uncertainty of income, especially in a gig economy where job stability is less guaranteed. People might also struggle with lifestyle inflation; as they earn more, they may find themselves spending more, thereby negating any savings efforts. High debt levels can act as an anchor, pulling individuals away from their goals. Furthermore, societal pressures and the desire to keep up with peers can lead to financially unwise decisions. Emotional hurdles, such as fear of investing or taking financial risks, can also play a significant role. The added complexity of balancing work with personal life responsibilities can create stress, making the FIRE (Financial Independence, Retire Early) journey seem overwhelming.

To build resilience against these setbacks, it's important to develop practical strategies that keep motivation high. Creating a clear, detailed plan for your financial journey can help. Break down larger goals into smaller, manageable tasks, making it easier to track progress and celebrate small victories. Regularly reviewing your situation can spark new ideas and encourage adaptive thinking. Establishing a support network of like-minded individuals can also provide encouragement and accountability. This could be in the form of online forums, local groups, or even close friends who share similar goals. In moments of doubt, remind yourself of your 'why'—the underlying motivation for pursuing FIRE. Staying connected to that motivation can provide a powerful boost during difficult times, helping to keep you on track towards financial independence.

Another useful tip is to maintain flexibility in your financial plan. Life is unpredictable, and being adaptable allows you to adjust your strategies as new challenges arise. For instance, if an unexpected expense occurs, consider ways to cut from non-essential areas of your budget without feeling deprived. Regularly reassessing your priorities can also help you stay aligned with your long-term goals, ensuring that you are always moving forward. Remember, the path to financial independence is a marathon, not a sprint. Staying focused on sustainable habits and utilizing community resources can go a long way in overcoming challenges on the road to achieving financial independence.

15. Continuous Financial Education

15.1 Resources for Ongoing Learning

Books and online courses are invaluable tools for anyone looking to expand their financial knowledge. Popular titles like The Total Money Makeover by Dave Ramsey offer practical advice on budgeting and debt elimination, making them a great starting point. For those interested in investing, The Intelligent Investor by Benjamin Graham deep dives into value investing principles that can help you navigate the stock market. Online platforms such as Coursera and Udemy offer courses ranging from personal finance fundamentals to advanced investment strategies; these resources can be tailored to your specific learning needs. Additionally, platforms like Khan Academy provide free courses that cover everything from basic financial literacy to sophisticated economic concepts, ensuring continuous learning at your own pace.

Engaging with podcasts and blogs can also keep your financial knowledge fresh and relevant. Podcasts like The Dave Ramsey Show offer real-life financial advice through listener questions, while BiggerPockets Money focuses on financial independence and real estate investing strategies. These podcasts not only educate but inspire listeners to take actionable steps towards financial stability. On the blogging front, websites like The Motley Fool provide analytical insights into stocks and investing trends. Similarly, NerdWallet offers articles that break down credit scores and budgeting tips in easily digestible formats. Following these resources keeps you updated on current trends and equips you with the knowledge needed to make informed financial decisions.

Remember to actively incorporate what you learn. Setting aside time each week for reading a chapter of a financial book or listening to a relevant podcast episode can transform your financial understanding over time. This consistent commitment to learning allows you to stay ahead, adapt to changes, and confidently manage your personal finances.

15.2 Importance of Staying Updated on Financial Trends

Monitoring financial news is essential for anyone looking to manage their personal finances wisely. Staying informed about economic changes and trends can significantly influence your financial decisions. Economic indicators, employment rates, inflation, and interest rates can all shift rapidly, affecting everything from your savings strategy to investment choices. By regularly consuming credible financial news, whether through reputable websites, podcasts, or financial analyses, you gain insights into market movements and government policies that could impact your financial situation. Understanding market trends helps you spot potential risks and opportunities, allowing you to react promptly to shifts that might affect your financial stability.

Adaptation strategies play a crucial role in effectively responding to changing market conditions. Learning how to tweak your financial plans based on fresh information is key to maintaining and enhancing your financial health. For instance, during inflationary periods, you might consider adjusting your investment portfolio to include assets that historically perform well in such environments, like commodities or real estate. Alternatively, if interest rates drop, refinancing loans could save you a significant amount of money. Developing a mindset geared towards flexibility enables you to pivot your financial strategies, ensuring you can take advantage of favorable market conditions while minimizing losses during downturns. The ability to adapt is not just beneficial; it is, in many cases, essential for achieving long-term financial goals.

To stay ahead, establish a routine of reviewing financial news at least a few times a week. This consistent engagement not only keeps you informed but also strengthens your ability to spot trends early, so you can adjust your finances accordingly. Keep an eye on financial reports and expert forecasts that address economic variables that matter to you, be it retirement planning, investment strategies, or budgeting techniques. Regularly revisiting your financial plan in light of new information can help you stay proactive rather than reactive, which is a smart way to navigate the complexities of personal finance.

15.3 Building a Network for Financial Growth

The world of finance can often feel overwhelming, but connecting with like-minded individuals can significantly enhance your financial literacy. Networking is not just about making contacts;

it's about forming relationships with financially-minded people who can share their insights and experiences. Engaging in discussions about money management, investment strategies, or budgeting techniques provides a supportive environment where you can learn and grow. These connections can introduce you to resources, tools, and ideas that you may not have encountered on your own. Often, having a mentor or simply a peer group to bounce ideas off can lead to breakthroughs in your understanding of complex financial concepts. Additionally, surrounding yourself with others who prioritize financial growth can inspire and motivate you to take actionable steps toward your own financial goals.

Joining financial groups can be a valuable strategy for anyone looking to enhance their personal finance knowledge. These groups and communities, whether online or locally, are focused on sharing tips, resources, and support among their members. Being part of such a community allows for continuous learning—members often share their success stories, challenges, and strategies that have worked for them, fostering a rich environment of shared knowledge. Moreover, many financial groups offer workshops, webinars, and seminars that cover a range of topics from budgeting basics to advanced investment techniques. This creates opportunities for practical learning and networking, which can often lead to collaborations or partnerships that further enhance your financial journey.

Remember, the connections you build today will pay dividends in the future. Set a goal to attend at least one financial seminar or networking event each month. This small step can lead to significant growth in your financial knowledge and network.

www.ingramcontent.com/pod-product-compliance
Lightning Source LLC
Chambersburg PA
CBHW062316220526
45479CB00004B/1195